GASTRIC BAND HYPNOSIS TECHNIQUES

LEARN HOW TO BURN FAT QUICKLY
AND BUILD STRONG AFFIRMATIONS
BY GAINING SELF-ESTEEM
THROUGH THE POWER OF
THE SUBCONSCIOUS MIND

GISELLA HERNANDEZ

There are no scenarios in which the publisher or the original author of this work can be in any fashion deemed liable for any hardship or damages that may befall them after undertaking information described herein.

Additionally, the information in the following pages is intended only for informational purposes and should thus be thought of as universal. As befitting its nature, it is presented without assurance regarding its prolonged validity or interim quality.

Trademarks that are mentioned are done without written consent and can in no way be considered an endorsement from the trademark holder.

TABLE OF CONTENT

Introduction

If you are trying to lose weight fast or just want to make sure that the weight is coming off as quickly and safely as possible, then it might be worth looking into gastric band hypnosis. This treatment may be a good option if you have tried other methods of weight loss but are not finding the results that you were hoping for. Gastric band hypnosis is also right for people who don't want to have stomach surgery in order to lose weight.

Gastric band hypnosis is a weight loss treatment in which a therapist will talk to you while you are in a state of deep relaxation. During this time, he or she will give you suggestions that will reprogram your subconscious mind. The goal of gastric band hypnosis is to make the patient feel full of fewer calories by changing the way that he or she thinks about food.

The average person who undergoes gastric band hypnosis loses around five pounds per month. Some people lose a lot more than this, and some lose less. The nice thing about gastric band hypnosis is that it allows a patient to have control over his or her weight loss. You can decide how quickly you want to lose weight and work with your therapist to make the process as safe and effective as possible.
In general, gastric band hypnosis is very safe. It does not involve any drugs or trauma to the body, and it will not damage any organs or result in any medical complications. There is also no need for surgery and no side effects are associated with getting this treatment.

Gastric band hypnosis is an option for people who have tried other forms of weight loss without success. It can also be a good choice if you don't want to have any type of surgery. However, gastric band hypnosis is not a perfect solution to every problem. For example, the start-up cost of this procedure may not be right for everyone. In addition, some patients may find that it works better for them than it works for their friends and family members.

Gastric band hypnosis is a good choice if you have tried other forms of weight loss and either found that they didn't work, or you didn't like the side effects. Gastric band hypnosis can also be a good fit if you do not want to have surgery and don't want to go through a lot of pain or torture in order to lose weight. However, gastric band hypnosis is not right for everyone since it might not work as well for some people as it does for others. Also, if you are interested in gastric band hypnosis, then make sure that your therapist has had the proper training and has used this treatment correctly.

When women start a healthy weight loss routine, they are bound to lose certain parts of their bodies faster than others. This is because of the different functions in men's and women's bodies and because of the difference in mass between men and women. Most often, a woman will lose weight faster from her midsection. This is what we also call belly fat or abdominal fat. Having a lot of this type of fat is not healthy because it is linked to diabetes, heart disease, and hypertension. Since women usually have more of this fat than men do, losing all or at least most of it will make them look and feel better.

However, the question now is: How can we accomplish that?

Studies show that gastric band hypnosis is a good way for women to lose belly fat and other types of excess weight around the body. This procedure was developed by Paul McKenna who was also known for his book I Can Make You Thin which has sold millions of copies in the UK. This treatment was designed to help women lose weight fast and all in a natural way.

This procedure can be used by both men and women, but it is more useful for women. Women have a lot of health problems, such as heart attacks, stroke, etc. This makes them vulnerable to medical complications which are not experienced by men. The chances of a woman having these diseases are higher than those of a man too. Hence the need to protect the heart and body when losing weight. It is for this reason that most hospitals have special units for obese females who need treatment from doctors specially equipped with handling these situations safely and effectively.

What is a Gastric Band?

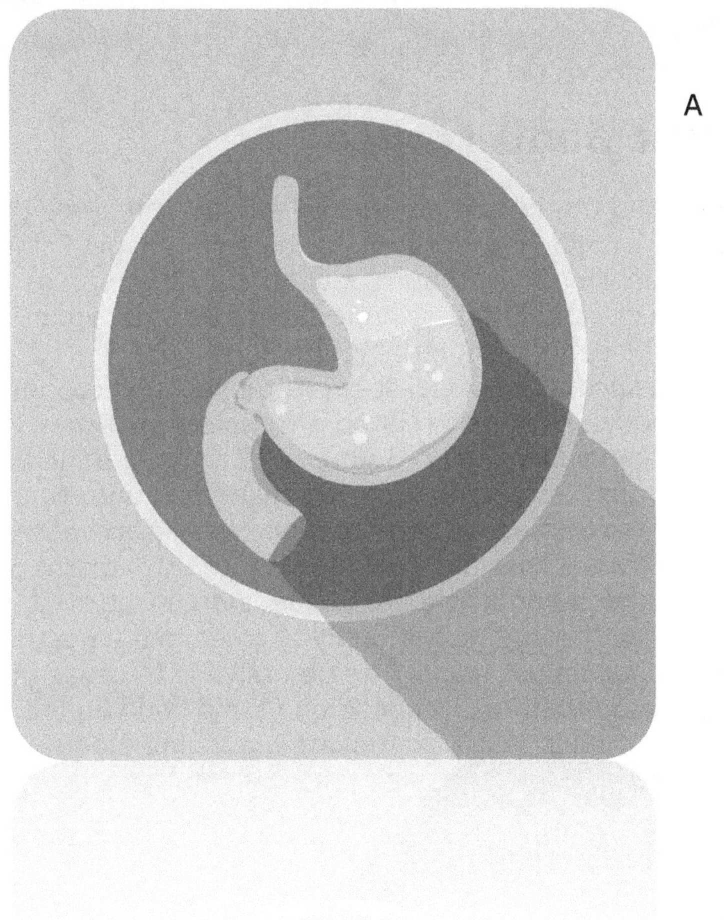

Stomach band is a silicone flexible apparatus utilized in weight reduction medical procedures. To create a modest pack over the gadget, the band is put around the upper part of the belly. This restrains the amount of sustenance that can be put away in the stomach area, making eating enormous amounts hard.
A gastric band will likely constrain the amount of sustenance that an individual can expend physically, making them feel full in the wake of eating next to no to advance weight reduction. It is a final hotel for most people

who have this medical procedure after endeavoring for other weight reduction systems. Like any medical procedure, there are perils in fitting a gastric band.

Gastric Band Trance

Gastric band trance can be utilized without the perils that accompany medical procedures to help people get thinner. A two-dimensional procedure is utilized by numerous trance specialists. The first hope to characterize your enthusiastic eating's underlying driver.
Utilizing trance, the specialist can urge you to recall long-overlooked nourishment-related encounters that may now influence you subliminally. Before performing gastric band hypnotherapy, tending to and perceiving any unfortunate reasoning, examples concerning sustenance can be helpful. Next, the trance specialist will play out the treatment of the virtual stomach band. The technique is proposed to recommend that you had an activity to embed a gastric band at a subliminal stage. The objective is to cause your body to respond to this proposition by making you feel quicker as though you were having a genuine medical procedure.

How am I going to feel afterward?

The general objective of the gastric band is to encourage a more beneficial nourishment association. If your subliminal thinks you have a gastric band fitted, your stomach will believe it's lower. This, thus, makes your mind send messages that, in the wake of devouring less nourishment, you are finished.

Perceiving when you are physically finished can be hard for the individuals who gorge. At times we eat only for taste (or comfort), overlooking whether we are physically ravenous or not. In developing smart dieting works on, figuring out how to perceive the physical vibes of being ravenous and being finished is helpful.

In contrast to gastric band medical procedures, there are no physical symptoms in the virtual gastric band. For a few, the real medical procedure may trigger the reflux of queasiness, regurgitating, and corrosive. Since mesmerizing, the gastric band is not a physical technique, it won't trigger such side effects.

The activity ought to be a charming and loosening up understanding, with most people revealing from entrancing an impression of quiet.

How Powerful Is Our Subconscious?

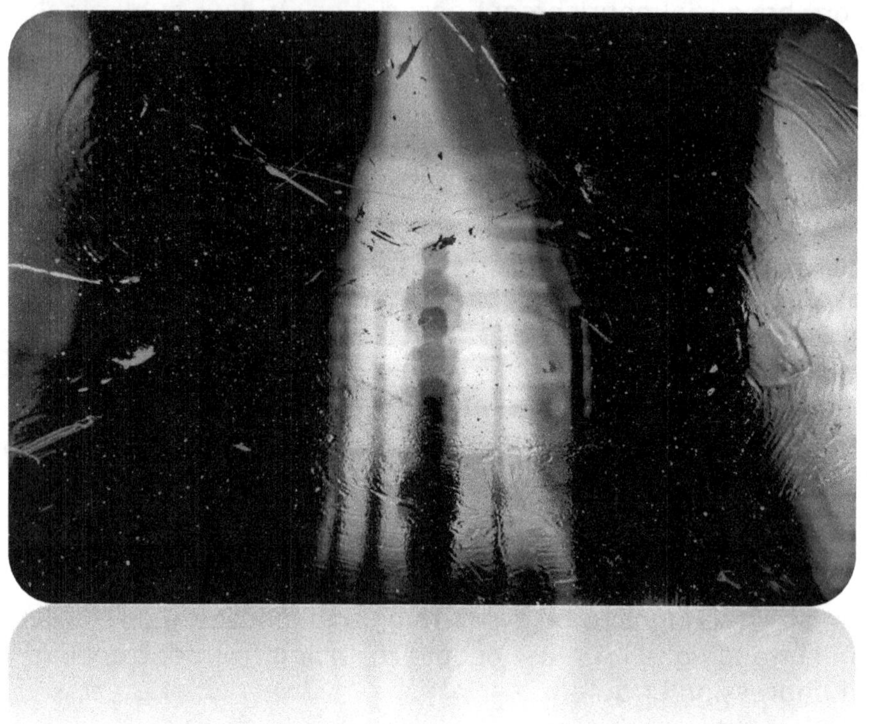

Grace's naturally magnificent charm and beauty brought her a complete scholarship to a prestigious modeling college. She fell out after six weeks because her weight ballooned to more than two hundred pounds, which stayed for another fifteen years regardless of persistent weight reduction attempts. Jack, fifty years older, was overweight since high school, even though playing sports, doing regular exercise, also creating many efforts at weight reduction. Whenever his weight starts to fall, he feels fearful until he regains the pounds.

Mary has won and gained the same twenty-five pounds throughout her adult life. She knows the routine and activates; however, she feels so helpless to alter them and shed the pounds once and for everyone. Alex is a

successful executive in a competitive tech industry that
always struggles with his burden.
He works hard, makes a higher income, and will multitask
better than many, but cannot restrain the size of the waist.
Ted has been CEO of a global source firm. His friends saw
him as he moved from being a photograph of wellness to
some health hazard due to excessive weight reduction.
Grace, Jack, Mary, Alex, along Ted, are actual cases we
found in treatment for weight loss with hypnosis.
Like many other people, these folks once believed that food
and eating were the issues causing their surplus fat. This
chapter is all about what they discovered are the genuine
culprit--the psychological mechanisms that affect or affect
eating and weight reduction. We'll have a look at how
inherent psychological problems are expressed in a way
that triggers and keep excess fat. We'll learn more about
using hypnosis to discover the use of feelings and burdens.
We're not likely to speak about eating disorders--like
bulimia, anorexia, and pica--or even other hurtful
behaviors. This chapter is about the most common
methods by which our bodies can gain weight and keep it
on.

The Mind-Body Mirror

Considering these are out of our mind-body medication practice, let's briefly examine a few of the standard methods that physical ailments are created by the mind-body. There are various examples where suppressed and repressed emotions locate saying by manifesting as physical symptoms and ailments.

Emotions and psychological conflicts that Aren't consciously acknowledged, voiced, or Provided voice mayor will be voiced from the body. Here's a pervasive case. When anger isn't recognized and expressed, it can lead to muscles in your head, neck, and shoulders tightening up and stressed, which causes a pressure headache. It is the literal manifestation of something or somebody that's a pain in the throat. Another individual experiencing the very same feelings of anger may be burning over the circumstance, also expertise nausea, nausea, or an illness.

Your skin is the organ that's quite responsive to feelings. Also, a state of urticaria (hives) may erupt whenever somebody is getting under their skin or rubbing them the wrong manner or any time the individual is itching to say or do something, or even any emotion is erupting into the surface.
Your emotions are emotions, such as happy, sad, or mad. If feelings or emotions aren't expressed, the mind-body will reflect them in imaginative ways.

Therapeutically, metaphors help us understand what the human body is expressing.
A figure of language or metaphor describing a psychological reaction like "a pain in the throat" is expressed through muscular strain and hassle, since the psychological frustration isn't being expressed differently. It can be a frequent encounter because, most times, it isn't okay or advisable to admit and convey anger or other emotions. For instance, if your boss embarrasses you or gets an unreasonable request, you can jeopardize your job if you have voiced your anger. Instead, you place it out of thoughts and go to another thing. Putting it from the mind doesn't place it from human anatomy.

Since you will notice from the hypnosis cases used in treatment, feelings and psychological conflicts could be placed out of thoughts, but not always from the body. You're able to suppress feelings or repress them. Suppressing feelings is if you intentionally decide not to consider them. Repressing emotions occurs whenever your subconscious does this without the advantage of choosing to perform it yourself. We'd love to spell out the difference between thoughts and feelings. Ideas are thoughts, beliefs, ideas, and conclusions on your own conscious or "thinking thoughts." Feelings or emotions are expressed in your entire body.

They arise in a crude place deep within the brain known as the limbic system. Both ideas and feelings are "items" in the meaning they're not only in your thoughts.

They involve power and chemistry, and they're transmitted and energetically throughout your nervous system along with other pathways inside the body. The chemical compounds called hormones, like dopamine, serotonin, noradrenaline, and acetylcholine, would be the common ones included.
If someone experiences mental sluggishness, then he can notice more psychological acuity if he comprises nuts, oatmeal, along with other choline-rich foods within his everyday decisions. Choline affirms the purposes of acetylcholine, which subsequently promotes memory and mental sharpness. We would like to highlight that these psychological and cognitive reactions and routines are real and happen to be analyzed for our purposes.

Feelings or emotions comprise pain, anxiety, guilt, despair, joy, anger, pleasure, bliss, contentment, serene, stress, and isolation. Notice that "poor" and "good" aren't from the record of feelings. Though we may say "I feel awful" or "I'm great," these aren't emotions. These are conclusions about what you believe; however, they aren't feelings. More correctly, if you create these announcements, you believe "I feel sick" or even "I feel well," which are approaches to explain how you're feeling, maybe not what you're feeling. Now, this is your only worth remembering: "Fat" isn't a feeling. Though folks say, "I feel fat," "fat" isn't a feeling.

Whenever someone says they're "feeling fat, then" it's a declaration about a feeling, like feeling fulfilled, filled, complete, or outside full. You could be thinking, "Why the big deal on the selection of words? I understand what I mean when I state that." The reason why we emphasize that is your feelings, as well as your voice about your emotions, are part of your own beliefs about yourself, and if you maintain these in understanding or talk them aloud, they're direct messages to your subconscious mind. Your mind-body finds all of it, and also long after it's from the mind (consciousness), it isn't from your own body's mind. You are going to want to select carefully what your goal will be to think and anticipate about your weight loss and exactly what and how you are feeling about it for it'll reflect it.

Saving Grace

One occurred to Grace that induced her to overlook her modelling college scholarship. She arrived at the office and expressed the desire to work with hypnosis to help her slim down. She clarified many different trials of weight loss methods that had been ineffective. Whenever she didn't lose fat, it'd return. She believed that there was "something" keeping her out of losing weight. In carrying her background, we discovered she had been thirty-six years older, married with three kids, ages eight, seven and five. Her weight was always over two hundred pounds for approximately fifteen decades. She grew up in the Midwest with a fantastic family and also had three sisters. Grace explained herself as the only woman in her household, having a weight issue. When asked regarding her weight record, she'd only say she "ate a lot." After finishing a thorough psychological and psychological evaluation, we proceeded to educate her about sculpting.

If she felt comfortable enough to move, we started with an induction method such as those on the sound with this publication. Grace relaxed readily into a trance country, wherein she had been absorbed in her thoughts and thoughts of a relaxing and enjoyable spectacle. As she pictured being on holiday with her loved ones, I provided hypnotic suggestions for her mind about letting her insight into the function or purpose of her extra body fat. In a couple of minutes, she seemed worried, and I asked her to explain what she was experiencing as she lasted.
She explained riding a train and also becoming the very first to arrive in the modelling school. The government office has been shut; however, a friendly janitor assisted her suitcases and unlocked the door to her delegated dining space. She was getting tearful and stressed as she continued talking. I assured her she would disrupt the squint at any moment or she would move more gradually and professionally. I informed her that she understood she had been at our office today as she recalled something

which happened afterward, fifteen decades back. Through her tears, she clarified the favorable janitor returning after that night, allowing himself to her chamber and hammering her.

The memory of the experience was rather exhausting and mentally draining for Grace. Discussing her following the trancework, I discovered it was nearly fifteen years since she'd thought about that adventure. She'd forgotten it. Initially, she opted to put this from her head, to curb this particular memory, but it had been put from her head so well that she'd forgotten that she forgot it. It had been repressed. She said this is the only real-time and location she had spoken to anybody about the encounter.

We spent a second session referring to her expertise in modelling faculty, and I requested her to earn some photos from this period. We used the photos to help her recall events so that she could chat about them at the security of treatment. She related that through the initial six months in school, her burden slowly improved, and she was anxious, fearful, embarrassed, depressed, and sleep-deprived. She didn't talk about the rape with anybody and moved home to wed her high school love.

He'd continuously accepted her for himself, and her burden was not a problem with him. Our counselling sessions demonstrated the goal of her excess body fat was a kind of defense. Her weight securely commanded her beauty so that she had been shielded from becoming the target of the following sexual assault. After she confessed, voiced, and revived the experience and feelings (fear, pity), Grace's weight loss plan was quite robust in cutting her dimension to wherever she felt joyful and secure. In her situation, we realize that the subconscious had been working out a role, and also there was a reason for the surplus weight.
It secured her and enabled her to feel secure. Though there was some time after she had been happy others found her appealing, the attack produced a panic that became linked to becoming captivating.

After analyzing these feelings and eliminating this anxiety, she had been free to discharge her additional weight and feel secure when she felt appealing.

24

Subconscious More Open To Suggestion During Hypnosis

If you are on a diet and have trouble sticking with it, there's help at hand. Hypnosis, one of the oldest ways of fighting obesity might just be the answer that you need. This article explains what hypnosis is and how it may help people to lose weight by giving them positive affirmations that they can listen to anytime they feel like slipping off their diet.

Hypnosis is one of the oldest ways to fight obesity - with good reason: this psychological therapy taps into your subconscious mind, where those feelings about overeating are stored.

As with dieting in general, rapid weight loss is not guaranteed with hypnosis, but it may be more effective for some people; furthermore, some lifestyle changes are advised to ensure that weight loss results become consistent.

Some research has shown hypnosis to be an effective form of weight loss. It has also been shown to be helpful for patients with conditions such as high blood pressure and stress-related illnesses. Theoretically, the body's responses to hypnosis could help reduce calorie intake by modifying appetite control mechanisms.

One study found that even if people were given a full night's sleep before weigh-ins, they still tended to put on the same amount of weight. It seems that the difference between being overweight and not is more about willpower than calories.

In the past, scientists believed that internal processes of your brain caused you to want to eat; it was not until recently that the idea of peripheral neural stimulation was introduced.

The most common type of hypnosis is focused on helping you eat less by making you more aware of your body's signals about hunger and fullness. Hypnotists also help you learn new behaviors and thought patterns that will make changes in your lifestyle easier to achieve.

Some research has shown that hypnosis is effective for weight loss, but there are not enough large-scale studies to determine exactly how much weight you can lose using hypnosis or how long it may take. Many people feel that they can control their eating habits, and if this is true for you, then you will probably be able to use the skills taught in hypnosis without any issues. However, if you have problems with food, then experts agree that proper help should be sought before beginning any form of rapid weight loss program. The biggest issue with rapid weight loss is getting enough nutrients; this is especially true in women because they need extra iron and calcium to avoid osteoporosis.

For some people, hypnosis can help them to overcome their fears associated with weight loss. As long as you are not afraid of letting go of the control you have over your eating habits, you are unlikely to have any problems.

This is supported by the fact that there is no medical evidence to support or comment on the effectiveness of hypnosis for rapid weight loss.

Preparation and training are essential when going through the hypnotic process; therefore, you may need a coach or therapist who can guide you through this as well as give suggestions throughout. For some patients, self-hypnosis may be enough; however, many people find that they need extra help from someone qualified to hypnotize them. A study published in the International Journal of Clinical and Experimental Hypnosis found that hypnosis is more successful for weight loss when it is done with a therapist than when you do it yourself.

How Do Physical Gastric Bands Differ from Gastric Band Hypnosis?

Physical gastric bands are typically used for patients who are morbidly obese. The surgery is performed by making an incision in the stomach and then placing a belt around it. This forces the stomach to empty slower, which means that patients feel fuller faster, so they eat less. It also makes them more likely to chew their food properly and not gulp it down too quickly.

Weight loss with a physical gastric band is usually very slow, taking up to three years to be complete- if ever! However, this does make the weight loss permanent because the patient has changed their eating habits rather than just focusing on dieting with food restrictions or expensive meal replacements like shakes or drinks.

In contrast, gastric band hypnosis (GBH) involves hypnotizing the patient about 10-12 weeks before surgery. This helps them to become more relaxed and reach a deep level of hypnotic trance where they can feel and hear things that are taking place in their bodies without opening their eyes. In this way, they're able to accept the operation much easier than if they were just told what was going to happen and had no idea how it would really feel afterward. Again, this makes the operation more permanent. The patient does not regain the lost weight easily (may have to do it for up to 10 years in this case) and there is no possibility of regaining it if they don't follow the operation's pre-occupations and dietary instructions.

The main message is that an individual will be able to lose more weight with physical gastric bands than with a procedure like gastric band hypnosis. GBH requires a lot of skill, so it will not be easy for most people to lose as much weight as they would have been able to with a simple physical gastric band.

An alternative to gastric band hypnosis is to do a combination of both procedures. The advantage of this would be to have a more permanent weight loss, but it does take a lot longer for the patient to reach a deep enough hypnotic state and achieve permanent weight loss than with an actual gastric band alone.

A patient is usually known by weighing themselves every day for the first month after surgery. Most patients will lose between 5-10% (about 10 kg) of their body weight within a month. This is because their bodies are still healing, and there's not enough food in the stomach to absorb. After three months, if they're losing around 1 kg a week, then it's likely that their body has accepted the operations and will not try to compensate by eating more. From here on, they can continue to lose

weight at a rate of about 0.5-1 kg per week until their target weight has been achieved (this depends on individual personal circumstances).

Researchers have found that patients who lose between 5-10% of their body weight as a result of physical gastric band surgery, are likely to keep it off for the rest of their lives. This is because the weight loss is permanent. After all, it's a change in eating habits rather than just dieting. This makes more sense than losing a huge amount of weight than trying to regain it, which is what happens with gastric band hypnosis.

In summary, physical gastric bands are effective and safe when used for patients who are morbidly obese. However, those who are not morbidly obese typically get much better results with gastric band hypnosis alone than they would if they were to have both procedures together.

Hypnotic Gastric Virtual Band

The virtual gastric band is a technique that combines hypnosis and subliminal reprogramming to make the stomach believe that it is smaller than it really is in order to reduce food intake and promote weight loss.
This type of treatment is based on the belief that obesity is a permanent problem so the patient has to learn to eat a balanced diet voluntarily and effortlessly to avoid the problem of the rebound effect. Through hypnosis, the patient receives messages of healthy routines that he will put into practice after the session.

Virtual gastric band procedure

This technique acts similarly to those of stomach reduction, limits the amount of food ingested to lose weight. To get the feeling of satiety without using any external device, the patient must attend a hypnosis session. When the patient is in a state of semi-unconsciousness, he will receive subliminal messages to decrease the desire to eat and adopt new healthier eating routines.
This procedure is based on psychological techniques of cognitive-behavioral therapy (CBT) to change habits must be reinforced from time to time. The messages are losing strength over time, especially in long treatments. Besides, to receive recordings that the patient will hear periodically, he must attend other hypnosis sessions to adapt the messages according to the moment he is in.
This technique acts like other stomach reduction procedures such as the gastric band, hence its name. The patient will take less food as the stomach will send the

satiety message to the brain before it is filled. The virtual gastric band can also be a complementary technique to other surgical treatments or not for stomach reduction, helping the patient to acquire the new routines without much effort.

Advantages and disadvantages

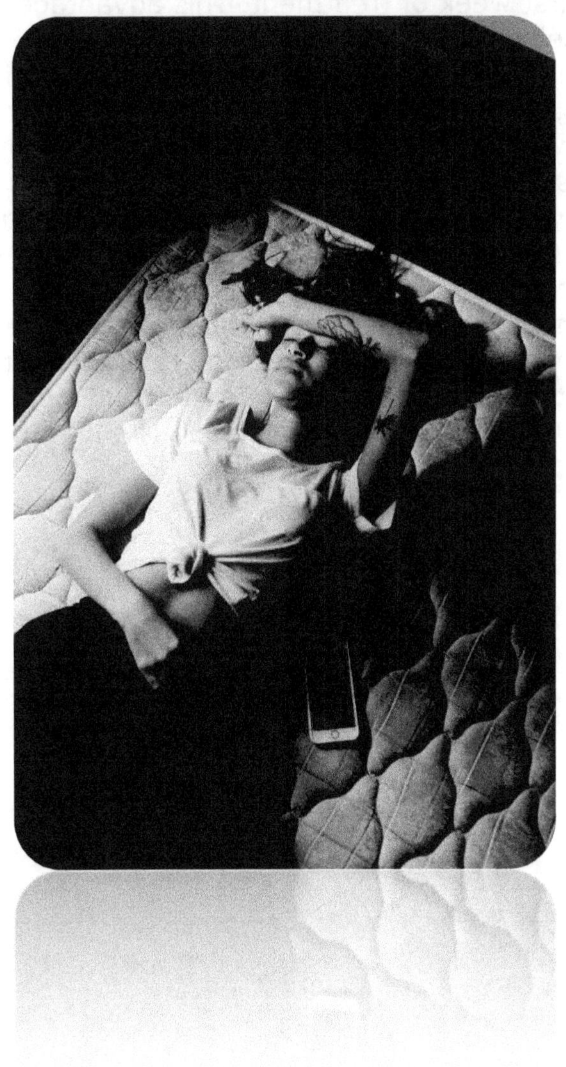

The main advantage offered by a virtual gastric band treatment is that there is no surgical intervention of any kind, it is a non-invasive treatment. Therefore, it does not require hospitalization, nor does it leave scars even if they are minimal.

Using a virtual gastric band treatment allows you to see results from the beginning. That is, the patient loses weight from the first week of treatment. This advantage favors the patient's self-esteem and strengthens the beliefs of the new routines.

In general, the cost of a virtual gastric band treatment is usually lower than that of other stomach reduction techniques.

However, virtual gastric band treatment is a relatively new technique for which there is not enough scientific evidence of long-term results.

In addition, it is necessary for the patient to have some implications because he must attend reinforcement sessions so that the subliminal messages do not lose strength. Weight gain in obese people is a long-term treatment.

Lose Weight with the Gastric Virtual Band

How many times have you considered losing weight? And how many others have you made a diet that you have abandoned because of the effort involved in getting rid of those extra pounds?
Have you ever raised that the causes are not only biological, that there must be psychological, emotional, or unconscious causes that make you continue to eat disproportionately or compulsively?
Ask yourself if you really want to lose weight and if so, we can propose a new, revolutionary and effective method, is the gastric virtual band with hypnosis.
A painless, risk-free, and easy method, as we provide it to you.

What is the virtual gastric band by the hypnosis method?

As you have read in the initial questions, and surely the answers have been many times referring to the first approach and concerning the second one, I am sure that you have also thought about it once but you do not find a connection, that is, how you could imagine that it is not that you eat for eating, but you often eat for anxiety, for frustration, for disappointment, for boredom, for comforting you, etc.…, in a nutshell: You eat your emotions.

It is at this last point that clinical hypnosis does its job since many behavior patterns, especially those related to food, are learned and automatic.

Through clinical hypnosis, we access the subconscious and create a series of suggestions to recreate an operation of a virtual gastric band that will allow the person to eat and notice satiety as if they had really operated on you, but without the side effects that may occur. Produce a real operation, since many people do not know how to physically identify the limit of their satiety.

Therefore, by implanting the gastric band through clinical hypnosis, the brain acts in the same way as if it were actually implanted since the mind believes it.

In the same way, we make a series of suggestions for each individual person to start eating naturally, without forcing anything, in a healthy and balanced way knowing when to stop and control for example when eating chocolate that does not eat all the box.

On the other hand and through another series of suggestions or hypnotic programming we make the person reduce or eliminate the desire that drives him to eat since normally the food he usually eats has many calories or sugar that later become fat and it is in extra kilos.

On the other hand, we create hypnotic suggestions to motivate people to move their body in any way, walking, exercising, but in such a way that these activities are carried out by people without that mental and physical effort that often involves them.

In some people, if necessary, we could find out through regressive clinical hypnosis if the causes of your overweight are related to some trauma or are the product of child behavior that you continue to perform as compensation or refuge from what is really affecting you and not solve.

In short, both through the implantation of the virtual gastric band by hypnosis and by issuing specific suggestions for each patient, we can get people to eliminate those kilos more definitively since at the end of the treatment we teach them a self-hypnosis technique so that they reinforce their new beliefs that emit so much with food, their figure thus achieving maintenance over time.

How Does Virtual Gastric Band Work

A virtual gastric band is presented as an alternative to diet slim. But how does it work? Each session consists of four sessions of 20 minutes each and follows four basic guidelines. The goal is to stop thinking about food all the time. It's simple in theory, but it can be a bit more difficult to do it logically. For simplicity, this method includes self-help advice, materials, and daily audio. In the second session, the stomach band is placed by hypnosis. There is no type of surgery, but due to hypnosis (which does not cause pain or imply any health risks or side effects), the subconscious believes that the stomach has a stomach band and behaves as if it were smaller). Therefore, you can eat less, feel fuller faster, and lose the kilos you need to reach your ideal weight.

Remember that food is often used for anxiety, boredom, or indifference. In this way, you eat from hunger, not from stress. This means that virtual stomach bands and mental control will not only save you kilos but will also adopt healthier eating habits. One of the goals of a slim diet is to retrain your habits when you eat.

The virtual gastric band method is specifically designed for those who want to lose a few pounds more and are overweight or obese, but also for people who can no longer lose weight while on a diet, or when food is a substitute for anxiety. On the other hand, it is not recommended for eating disorders (anorexia or bulimia), diabetes, or irritable bowel syndrome.

How to Find The Focus?

How to find the focus needed for gastric band hypnosis rapid weight loss for women?

1. Focus on yourself or those things that matter the most to you. Some people do not usually have a constant partner who will always be by their side during the ups and downs of their weight loss journey. If you are the type that does not have the support of a partner to encourage and motivate you, then this is good as long as it is not a problem for you. You can still focus all of your energy on reaching your goals.

2. Focus on your goals and be determined. This means that you should do your research and understand what it takes to achieve your goal effectively. Know what needs to be done first before turning to techniques such as gastric band hypnosis rapid weight loss for women. You should also set up a reasonable schedule and know how much time you will spend studying or working towards weight loss each day.

3. Do not quit if you fall behind in your weight loss journey at times. Everyone has his or her own challenges in life. Sometimes you will feel like giving up as you see your weight not going down, but you should also remember to take it one day at a time.

4. Find the best support that you can get from friends and family. Surround yourself with people who believe that you can do it and who are willing to help motivate and encourage you when needed. Take advantage of them by asking for help when needed and accept their good intentions.

5. Get yourself a job that allows you to work from home if possible so that there will be fewer distractions for you while trying to lose weight.

6. Have the right attitude that will help you to reach your goal. Try not to be too stressed out when it comes to your weight loss journey. You should have a positive attitude that will help you focus and motivate you.

7. Eat healthy foods at regular intervals throughout the day so that you do not skip meals and go without eating meals completely. All of these things will positively affect your progress in losing weight even if there is a setback or fall off in progress sometimes every now and then.

What are some excuses for not losing weight effectively?

There are many reasons why people fail to lose weight effectively even with gastric band hypnosis rapid weight loss for women. Some of these include:
- Lack of motivation. It is okay if you do not always feel motivated to lose weight as long as you do not make an excuse to stop doing so. If you think that it is normal for you to be lazy, then this is not a good reason for giving up. You should stay focused and stick with the plan until it is fully achieved.
- Excuses about food. This means that you have the wrong attitude when it comes to food and how much should be

eaten at any given time. You should always be aware of what foods to eat at what times especially during meals and snacks or when drinking sodas or juice during the day.
- Depression. If you are feeling depressed, you should allow yourself some time to work it out. Do not let depression make you give up on your weight loss plans. Try to find a way to escape the depression and move on with your life.
- Finishing off food or eating leftovers. You should only do so if there is no other choice, especially during parties or family gatherings. However, you should try to avoid this as much as possible and take leftovers home instead of finishing them off at the dinner table where they were originally served.

What Is Self-Hypnosis?

Self-hypnosis is a powerful method in which you talk right to the subconscious mind or part of your brain. It gives you a way to eliminate any obstacles and confusion within the dialogue of your mind-body.

Self-hypnosis is still considered a mystical phenomenon by many people, even though this technique can be seen as prayer. You are alone, and you concentrate on your well-being. If you like, you ask God or a supreme being you believe in to help you. This practice also includes meditation (just like praying does), as well as chanting, mantras, inner confirmation, or affirmation. When you have to perform at work or college, you make such statements like "I don't fear; I'm fine"; "I can do it" or exactly the opposite, like "I can't do it. Everybody is better than me," etc. Even when we imagine ourselves in a different scenario from what is currently happening, we are programming ourselves. What you are doing is continuously hypnotizing yourself. Self-hypnosis helps us to come into contact with the unconscious through the use of a specific language, aimed at awakening some parts of ourselves by leveraging archetypal symbols. Self-hypnotization is self-programming. Our unconscious understands the symbolic messages of words rather than their rational meaning; that's why figurative language is used in hypnosis for inducing the individual to relax and to focus on the inner world. We are embedding a vivid, information-rich image with emotions in the subconscious mind.

However, we must learn to pray, or let's say hypnotize ourselves accurately! Self-hypnosis is the ability to apply techniques and procedures alone to stimulate the unconscious to become our ally and involve it directly in the realization of our goals. By learning the essential elements of communication with the unconscious mind, it is possible to become able to reprogram activities of our unconscious. Self-hypnosis is a method that does not dismiss the support of a professional but has the advantage of being able to be performed independently. This is possible through the use of CDs and DIY courses made by hypnotists to make this practice accessible to a larger number of people with significant advantages, even from an economic point of view!

It is merely a process of moving variables; you become the inductee of the relaxed state and the one who suggests the positive ideas for change on yourself. You are both the guide into the relaxed state and the one experiencing the relaxed state. While this might seem like it ups the ante and makes the process much more complicated just by increasing your number of roles and responsibilities, it is much simpler than you could ever imagine.

What is Self-Hypnosis For?

It was Milton H. Erickson, founder of modern hypnotherapy, who gave an exhaustive illustration of the effects and purposes of hypnosis and self-hypnosis. The scholar stated that this practice aims to communicate with the subconscious of the subjects through the use of metaphors and stories full of symbolic meanings (Tyrrell, 2014).

If incorrectly applied, self-hypnosis can certainly not harm, but it may not be useful in attaining the desired results, with the risk of not feeling motivated to continue a constructive relationship with the unconscious. However, to do it as efficiently as possible, we need to be in a relaxed state of mind. So, accordingly, we start with relaxation to gather the attention inside, while suspending conscious control. Then we insert suggestions and affirmations to the unconscious mind. At the end of the time allocated for the process, a gradual awakening procedure facilitates the return to the state of permanent consciousness. When you are calm, your subconscious is 20-25% more programmable than when you are agitated. Also, it effectively relieves stress (you can repair a lot of information and stimuli you understand), aids regeneration, energizes, triggers positive physiological changes, improves concentration, helps you find solutions, and helps you make the right decisions. If the state of conscious trance is reached, then if the patient manages to let himself go by concentrating on the words of the hypnotist, progressively forgetting the external stimuli, the physiological parameters undergo considerable variations. The confirmation comes from science, and in fact, it was found that during hypnosis, the left hemisphere, the rational one,

decreases its activity in favor of the more creative
hemisphere, the right one (Harris, n. d.).
You can do self-hypnosis in faster and more immediate
ways, even during the course of the various daily activities
after you have experienced what state you need to reach
during hypnosis.
A better understanding of communication with the
unconscious mind highlights how indispensable our
collaboration is to slip into the state outside the ordinary
consciousness. In other words, we enter an altered state of
consciousness because we want it, and every form of
hypnosis, even if induced by someone else, is always self-
hypnosis.
We wish to access the extraordinary power of unconscious
creativity; for this, we understand that it is necessary to
put aside for a while the control of the rational mind and let
ourselves slip entirely into relaxation and into the magical
world of the unconscious where everything is possible.
Immense benefits can be obtained from a relationship that
becomes natural and habitual with one's own unconscious.
Self-hypnosis favors the emergence of constructive
responses from our being, can allow us to know ourselves
better, helps us to be more aware of our potential, and
more able to express them and use them to foster our
success in every field of possible application.

How Self-Hypnosis Works?

We all want time to just relax, dream, pretend. It refreshes the physical body and rejuvenates the spirit. It gives us just that when we practice our hypnosis: a very personal moment to enliven and be able to enrich our mind and body. The procedure is literally over. You need nothing more than a secure and comfortable venue.

Simple Rules

There are certain guidelines for hypnosis, and they make sure the practice is the most effective and has the greatest advantages. Find a convenient and quiet spot in your home or office when you're ready to start using the audio, where you can sit in a chair, recline or even lie down. Make sure you're comfortable, and you don't have to pay attention to anything else in a spot. Do not listen to your work on trance while driving a car or running some form of machinery. In order to practice your self-hypnosis properly, it is helpful to agree on a daily time each day or night. Bedtime is a perfect opportunity to enjoy your job in a trance, and training at this time can be a wonderful way to reach a restful sleep.

Distractions and interruptions are possible. Using them instead of making them torment you and drive you away from your job in a trance. To enhance your experience of trance, use the sounds in the environment around you. For example, you might hear a sound while doing your hypnosis, and start thinking that this sound distracts you. You then concentrate more on the diversion than on your hypnosis. You may be tempted to fight it — which takes energy off the hypnosis. Instead, when you notice a sound that appears distracting or annoying at first, take control of it by giving it your permission as a background sound to be here, giving it a task, for example by saying that "the barking dog's sound makes me go deeper and deeper inside" or "the fan motor sounds like a waterfall that's a soothing background tone." In our private practice in Tucson, there's a day school that always lets the kids play during one of our hypnosis sessions. That is when we say, "Children's sound can be a background sound that helps you to go deeper and deeper into yourself now." This is part of our philosophy of "using all."
Distractions also include the feelings you can feel in yourself. You may find yourself feeling, for example, a part of your body that itches. The more you focus on itching, or scratching the itch, the less you concentrate on the trance. You are just reminding yourself at those times that you have permission to move your attention back to your trance or daydream and let the itch go unravel. We teach patients a similar way of focusing attention away from the "distraction" of pain when working with them. If you have trouble letting go of an annoying distraction, you may need to order it to be there as a background sound or feeling, allowing you to go inside more comfortably. Detach yourself from anything your commitment to your hypnosis is competing with. Let go of any dispute with the world. Just let it be there and you won't notice it again sooner or later. Once you learn to accept a feeling, a noise, or

another factor that interferes with your hypnosis, you don't let it affect you any longer.

The Law of reversed effect

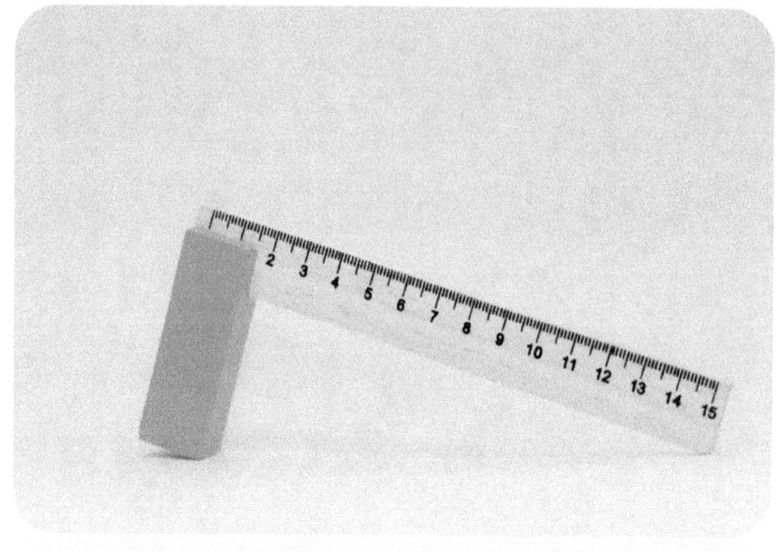

There is a law in hypnosis, called the Reversed Effect Law, which says that the more you sometimes try to do something, the more it doesn't happen. An example is when you want to say a name that you think you know—it may be a title to a book, a person, a movie—but at that moment you can't say it, and the more you try, the less it is there. The name comes when you say "I will remember later" or "It will come to me later," to your subconscious mind. By letting go of the question "What is the name? What name is it? "You activated your subconscious mind to get the answer right now, and it always does. So, the Reversed Effect Rule is that it just gives you the opposite (the reverse) when you are working too hard for it.

Simple procedures

Becoming absorbed in your thoughts and ideas is that gentle journey into the center of yourself called "going into a trance." Simple self-hypnosis techniques include going into a trance, deepening the trance, using that state of trance to give the mind-body messages and suggestions, and coming out of trance.

How To Identify The Root Cause Of Your Emotional Eating

Whether You're pleased with your body fat or not, it's what it is, accept your present weight is a direct outcome of your lifestyle habits, namely the quantity and kind of food and beverage you like and your routine exercise habits and activity levels.

A whole lot of bad eating habits are due to emotional eating; this is if our ingestion is ordered by how we're feeling, and we work with food to help us feel better. This is also referred to as relaxation eating, and generally entails excessive snacking or binging fatty foods that are fatty.

Emotional eating is a massive problem for a lot of men and women who struggle with their weight and typically highlight a poor men relationship with food. You may just break the custom of emotional eating should you determine what causes one to bite in this fashion; you need to discover the feelings and situations that cause you to lose control of your eating habits. Eating for comfort to cheer up yourself can develop into a vicious circle since you are able to become more miserable as you pile weight, forcing you to flip into food and make things worse (so it goes).

Here are a number of the usual triggers that could let you eat too much on a normal basis:

- Stress.

- Inadequate self-esteem.

- Depression.

- Boredom.

- Loneliness.

- Unhappy with your own body form.

- Marital or relationship problems.

- Financial worries.

- Deficiency of energy and inactivity.

- Greed.

People Rarely meet their emotional needs with a fresh green salad or even excessive quantities of fruit. Emotional eating normally involves consuming copious quantities of crap and convenience foods and candy snacks like chocolate and cake. Let's examine a few strategies that can help you manage your relationship with food and prevent you from binge eating.

Stress

Ever see how stress causes you to be hungry? It is not only on your mind. If stress is chronic, as it so often is in our hectic, rapid universe, your body generates elevated levels of the stress hormone, cortisol. The more rampant stress in your lifetime, the more inclined you should turn into food for emotional relief.

Stuffing emotions

Eating is a method to Silence temporarily or "things down" uncomfortable emotions, such as anger, anxiety, despair, anxiety, loneliness, bitterness, and shame. As you're numbing yourself with meals, you can prevent the difficult emotions you would rather not believe.

Boredom or feelings of emptiness

Do you eat just to give Yourself something to do, to alleviate boredom, or as a means to fulfill a void in your life? You truly feel unfulfilled and empty, and meals are a way to occupy your mouth and your own time. At the present time, it fills you up and distracts you from inherent feelings of purposelessness and dissatisfaction with your life.

Childhood customs

Think back to your own youth Memories of meals. Can your parents reward good behavior with ice cream, just take you out for pizza once you have a fantastic report card, or even give you candies if you're feeling unhappy? These customs may often carry over into adulthood. Or your ingestion might be driven by nostalgia--for precious memories of grilling hamburgers in the backyard with your father or drinking and baking snacks with your mother.

Childhood growth

For many people, emotional eating is A learned behavior. Throughout childhood, their parents provide them snacks to help them cope with a challenging day or scenario, or as a reward for something great. As time passes, the kid who reaches a cookie following a bad grade on evaluation might grow to be a grownup who catches a box of biscuits after a demanding day on the job. For instance, like this, the roots of emotional eating are heavy, which may cause breaking the habit incredibly challenging. Sometimes, people may eat so as to adapt; for instance, people could be told "you've got to complete your plate," and also, the person may eat beyond the point where they feel fulfilled.

Social influences

Getting along with other Men and Women To get a feast is a decent method to ease stress, yet it could likewise prompt indulging. It's anything but difficult to enjoy on the grounds that the food is there or essentially in light of the fact that every other person is eating. You could likewise gorge on social circumstances from nervousness. Or then again perhaps your family or friend network spurs you to gorge, and it is significantly simpler to go all together.

Negative impact

Negative affectivity is a character quality including negative feelings and insufficient self-idea. Negative feelings experienced in negative impacts contain outrage, blame, and tension. It's been found that specific unfriendly effect guideline scales called enthusiastic eating. An inability to pronounce and recognize the emotions made the person feel inadequate at controlling negative impact and thus more inclined to participate in emotional eating as a way for coping with these negative emotions. Further scientific research concerning the relationship between negative affect and ingestion uncover that, after undergoing a stressful event, food intake is associated with decreased feelings of adverse effect (i.e., Feeling awful) for individuals enduring high levels of chronic stress. This relationship between feeling and eating better indicates a self-reinforcing hierarchical pattern involving elevated levels of chronic stress and the consumption of highly palatable foods as a working mechanism. Contrarily, research conducted by Spoor et al. Discovered that negative affect isn't significantly linked to emotional eating, but both are associated through emotion-focused coping and avoidance-distraction behaviors. Though the scientific consequences differed somewhat, they suggest that adverse influence does play a part in emotional eating. However, it might be accounted for by other factors.

Connected Ailments

Emotional eating as a Way to deal Might be a precursor to developing eating disorders like binge eating or bulimia nervosa. The relationship between emotional eating as well as other ailments is large because of how emotional eating and those ailments share key attributes. All the more explicitly, they're similarly connected with feeling-centered adapting, maladaptive adapting systems, alongside a ground-breaking antipathy for negative feelings and incitement. It's very important to say that the causal management hasn't been established, meaning that although emotional eating is thought to be a precursor to those eating disorders, in addition, it might be the result of those ailments. The last hypothesis wherein enthusiastic eating occurs in response to some other eating malady is upheld by research, which has uncovered passionate eating to be basic among individuals previously experiencing bulimia nervosa.

Biological And environmental variables

Stress impacts food tastes. Quite a few research -- given, many of these in creatures have demonstrated that physical or emotional distress raises the consumption of food high in sugar, fat, or even in the absence of metabolic shortages. Once ingested, fat- and - sugar-filled foods appear to get a feedback effect that combats stress-associated reactions and emotions since these foods activate dopamine and opioid releases, which protect from the unwanted effects of stress. These foods actually are "comfort" foods because they appear to counteract stress, but rat studies reveal that occasional access to consumption of those highly palatable foods generates symptoms that resemble opioid withdrawal, implying that high fat and high-sugar foods may get neurologically addictive a couple of examples in the American diet could include: burgers, pizza, French fries, sausages, and salty pastries. The most typical food tastes are in decreasing order from candies energy-dense meals, non-sweet energy-dense food afterward, vegetables, and fruits. This may bring about people's stress-induced craving for all those foods.

The stress reaction is a Highly-individualized response, and individual differences in physiological reactivity can also result in the evolution of emotional eating customs. Girls are somewhat more prone than men to resort to eating as a coping mechanism for stress, as are overweight people and people with histories of dietary restraint. In 1 study, girls were subjected to an hour-long social stressor activity or even a neutral control condition. The women were subjected to every condition on various days. Following the actions, the girls were invited to a buffet with healthy and unhealthy snacks. People who had elevated chronic stress rates and very low cortisol reactivity to the intense stress task consumed more calories out of chocolate cake compared to women with reduced chronic stress levels following both control and stress conditions. High cortisol levels, together with higher sugar levels, might be accountable for stress-induced ingestion, as research suggests high cortisol reactivity is associated with hyperphagia, an abnormally enhanced desire for meals, during stress. Additionally, because glucocorticoids trigger hunger and especially increase one's desire for high fat and high-sugar foods, those whose adrenal glands normally exude larger amounts of glucocorticoids in reaction to a stressor are somewhat more likely toward hyperphagia. Furthermore, people whose bodies need more time to clean the blood of excess glucocorticoids are likewise predisposed.

These biological variables can Interact with environmental components to additionally activate hyperphagia. Regular intermittent stressors activate recurrent, irregular releases of glucocorticoids in periods too short to permit a comprehensive return to baseline levels, resulting in elevated and sustained levels of desire. Thus, those whose lifestyles or professions involve regular intermittent stressors over extended intervals thus have a higher biological incentive to come up with routines of emotional eating, which places them at risk for long-term undesirable health effects like weight reduction or cardiovascular disease.

The rationale is supporting stressful Ingestion: (1) emotional charge of food selection, (2) emotional reduction of food consumption, (3) impairment of cognitive consumption controllers, (4) ingestion to modulate emotions, and (5) emotion-congruent modulation of ingestion. These are split into subgroups of Dealing, reward improvement, societal, and conformity purpose. Therefore,

providing a person with is a stronger comprehension of
personal emotional eating.

57

Unhealthy Relationships With Food

Too often we eat too much of what we need, and this can lead to unwanted weight gain.

Careful eating is important because it will help you appreciate food more. Instead of eating large portions to feel full, you will try each bite.

This will be easy for those who want to do it fast but need to do something to increase their willpower by extending the periods between their hours. It will also be very useful for people who struggle with food.

Controlling a portion alone may be enough for some people to see the natural results of their weight loss plan. Try your best to incorporate careful eating practices into your daily life so you can control how much you eat.

This meditation will be specific to eating an apple. You can practice careful eating without meditation, share your meals with others, or sit alone with a nice view out the window. This meditation will guide you to understand the types of thoughts that will be helpful while staying alert during meals.

Change your Mindset

The first step you must take on your weight loss journey is to change your mindset. This is the first and very important step to sustainable weight loss.
As you work to change your weight loss mindset, you are, in effect, rethinking what you really believe about losing weight, so that your overall weight loss journey serves you better.

In other words, you need to cultivate your own weight loss condition. This psychological change you must take can be even more difficult than adding a few additional herbs to your plate.
This is a thing that needs to be done. First of all, be aware that there are three words to keep in mind when embarking on this journey.
These words are "I can't", "I won't," and "I can't". These are three short words that you must ban to be successful, as they come from your mind and have virtually nothing to do with your inner strength or what you can achieve.
If you use them frequently, they can have a huge indirect effect on your weight loss journey and your level of fitness. Therefore, you must reverse the entire scenario and leave the negative discussion behind. People trying to lose weight generally say so not just because of their past negative experiences.
For example, someone who says they don't like vegetables simply remembers old experiences that have nothing to do with their current behavior.
For this reason, their old experiences should not dictate their current behavior. If there are some that I can't or can't define in your vocabulary, you have to turn the script upside down and turn them into me and I can.
This will motivate and encourage you to go further and after several days you will be able to choose your new rhythm with ease.
If your current fitness level is low, the words "I can't" will hinder your success. Instead of saying I can't do ten push-ups, let's just say I'm trying to succeed. You have to try, as it is better to try and fail than fail.
You can start with two push-ups and with each new day add one more push to go further until you reach your fitness goal.
Your weight loss journey should start by changing your mindset and rewriting your thinking to lose weight
There are many natural ways to overcome your weight loss plateau, such as changing your eating habits and being physically active.

However, without changing your mindset, these tricks will only work in the short term by providing a sustainable weight loss journey, as there is always an underlying thought that keeps you away from sustainable weight loss. If you don't go there and face it, you will continue fighting along the way. For example, many women tend to lose weight as soon as they begin to make healthier dietary choices, but their weight loss progresses to a halt before they are completely satisfied with what they see in the mirror.

The truth is that losing weight sustainably is much more than losing those extra kilos that seem to melt at the beginning of the journey.

The trick is to keep losing weight after this initial period. Many women fail at this step because, after periods of weight loss, their progress simply freezes.

The key reason for this to occur is that the very common weight-loss plateau prevents you from losing weight in the long run.

To overcome this problem, there is no magic trick you can do other than changing your weight loss mindset.

Overcome Your Weight Loss Plateau

The secret to overcoming your weight loss plateau is not in a secret diet plan or training program, but it is much deeper in your mind.
The first step you need to take to overcome your weight loss plateau is to identify the real reasons why you are overweight.
If you're overweight, the main reason is probably not a lack of exercise, but a lack of willpower or dietary choices.
Yes, these are all the factors that determine your weight and play an important role in your overall health, how your body looks and feels.
Though, these are the only certain manifestation of the deeper, real reason behind your weight struggles.
For instance, those fat resources in the bodywork as some kind of body protection. When we accumulate fat, we, in fact, build a massive fat shield in order to protect the body from various kinds of threats.
Moreover, many of us struggle with different fears, many of us feel threatened all the time both subconsciously and consciously. In these cases, the fat we accumulate may serve as a hiding point making us less visible and making us less noticeable, less shiny in the world.
Many individuals feel greatly disappointed in some areas of their lives, many of them feel as if they are not following any certain life purpose.
Some of them are also greatly unsatisfied with their personal relationships and they feel no real connection with friends and family members.
These people struggling with threats and disappointments tend to hide behind their bodies and tend to fill their inner void by turning to food.
The truth is that there are many other psychological reasons for your weight struggles other than your dieting choices and your lack of physical activity.
As you work on changing your mindset, it is extremely important that you also work on identifying those reasons.

You must discover what is holding you back in order to get rid of those additional pounds for good.

64

Accept Current Reality

The next step requires that you truly accept your current reality. There are many females completely obsessing over their dieting plan, obsessing over counting calories, blaming their slow metabolism, and wondering what went wrong.

This is extremely unhealthy bringing nothing good. In fact, thinking obsessively about weight loss, hating what you see in the mirror, and thinking that your life would be much enjoyable if that excess fat were only a certain manifestation of the true thing that is keeping you from moving towards your goals.

Obsessing over these things, just shows that you are not accepting of your reality, that you resist it, and whatever you try to resist, it surely persists.

In order to overcome your weight loss plateau and to shred that stubborn excess weight, the first thing you are expected to do is to accept your current reality and work towards being okay with that.

This does not mean that you will stop your weight loss progress, but it means that by accepting your current reality, you can work towards a slimmer you in the future. Once there, you will be completely free of those relative internal tensions which, once gone, make you more focused and motivated to keep reaching your goals.

Find Your Motivation

Many people, when thinking about the motivation for weight loss, what comes to mind is those media motivational weight loss posters with skinny models repeating washed out phrases we have heard many times before with no personal message.

These types of weight loss motivational posters are extremely superficial and, in many cases, even damaging. Yes, they can motivate you for a short time period, but in the long run, this is not the kind of motivation you need to keep going.

Instead, you need to ask yourself what should be your own, your motivation without being conditioned by mass culture and media and their assumptions that being fit and skinny is what makes us happy and what makes our lives whole.

These assumptions in the majority of cases are not conscious at all and you should avoid them. Instead of resorting to mass culture and media, think about what is

truly important to you, what your inner senses and connection are telling you.
Think about what you want to gain with your weight loss. Is it being full of energy or being completely confident in what you see in the mirror?
In pursuance of discovering your true weight loss motivation, you need to examine how you truly feel, you need to work on addressing your core values, and finally take complete ownership over your life vision.
Your motivation must come from you as your unique, personal manifesto, not from some fitness magazine or workout poster you see.
Once you have identified your own weight loss motivation, you need to embrace your core value and let your own, personal vision in addition to your desired feelings, guide you towards reaching your goals.

This kind of motivation comes from within you is the only right motivation you need and once you have it, everything else will come naturally.

Virtual Gastric Band Treatment

The virtual gastric band treatment is a new approach to the problem of morbid obesity. It combines elements of cognitive therapy and hypnosis with a technique called psychosomatic relaxation. The technique takes advantage of the natural tendency for obese people to feel hungry after eating and full after they have fasted. The goal is to use relaxation exercises and physical sensations as a distraction during meals, causing feelings of fullness sooner, which should lead to eating less at each mealtime. The treatment is aimed at people who have tried and failed at diets or already had weight-loss surgery. It aims to help them reduce their food intake by 50%. The treatment is designed for people who have been deemed suitable for this kind of treatment. ?

What does virtual gastric band treatment entail?

The first step towards a virtual gastric band treatment usually involves a psychosomatic relaxation exercise. This step involves an awareness training program. It takes about three months to complete. You will be taught techniques like how to relax your body, how to relax your breathing and how to calm down your mind. You will also be told about techniques to cope with the emotional stresses in your life. You will also be taught how to go through a day without food, how to keep going when you are hungry and how to handle moments where you feel like giving up.

After that stage of the treatment, you will move on to the next step, which is the actual virtual gastric band treatment. This involves wearing a belt that has a device stuck between your stomach muscles (intragastric balloon). The device holds back part of your stomach so that it feels fuller for a longer period of time after eating. You will be connected to a machine that monitors how well the belt is working. This device is usually worn for 12 hours a day for six weeks in total.

The virtual gastric band treatment offers a new kind of approach in the fight against obesity. It combines three different approaches: hypnosis, cognitive therapy, and psychosomatic relaxation techniques. The combination of these three approaches has proven to be very effective in helping obese people lose weight.

At first, there was one researcher who thought about this new idea, Professor Bob Bloomfield, from Leeds Metropolitan University. As he explains in an interview:

The initial idea was to create a device that was invented by the gastric band and gastric bypass surgery, which is just a restriction device. So we wondered whether that would work. We asked people to wear them. The second thing, we got a lady hypnotist and we tried hypnotherapy. Then the third thing, the idea occurred to me that you could train people to use relaxation methods themselves.'

However, he admits that it took considerable time for his team of researchers to get this treatment going productively:

'This is not gold-plated stuff. You know, no one's making any money out of it whatsoever. I mean, it's a legal framework to bring it forward. You know, if we haven't made progress by the time, we've finished this degree of the research then we can't possibly get through a full university. That's the reason for this dip into hypnosis and hypnotism.'

In 1997 Bob Bloomfield and his co-researchers completed their research on the virtual gastric band treatment at Leeds Metropolitan University. They published their results in a medical journal called Diabetology and Metabolism.

The article was accepted but then vanished from the journal altogether because of an error that was only discovered in 2013 - more than two decades after it was written.

In 2013, the article was reprinted in the British Medical Journal Open, with an apology from the editor for overlooking it all those years ago.

The paper presented the results of 15 patients who had undergone hypnosis or cognitive therapy using the virtual gastric band treatment. Of those 15 patients, 13 lost weight, and 12 of them were able to keep it off for a year after their treatment. The average weight loss was 10% in 6 weeks. One of the study's participants lost 30 lbs and kept off 100 lbs. for four years after taking part in this virtual gastric band treatment.

The study also explored the relationship between mind and body in a way that could benefit both obese people and people with diabetes. A lot of the participants in this study had diabetes as well. The patients who went into the hypnosis sessions lost more weight than those who went through cognitive therapy alone. Hypnosis helped them to curb their cravings, while cognitive therapy helped them to think about food differently.

Patients in this study had been suffering from morbid obesity for at least 2 years and they had failed to keep their weight off after diets. One man in the study said:

'I've tried every diet going but I've never got anywhere on them. I always just came back to my old ways of eating. I thought, if this causes any weight loss, then that's positive, but in the meantime, I've been gaining weight anyway.'

One of the patients in the study explained how she lost more than 50 lbs:

'I could really feel it taking effect. I felt like a different person. Every week when I went for a checkup, without fail it would be up a few more pounds... It started with ten pounds and by the end of the month, I'd lost 20lbs. The hypnotist told me that if I could keep doing it like that every week then pretty soon, I would have lost all my excess weight. That would have been fantastic, but I didn't manage it. But I did come back every week, and when they took the band off at my final check-up at five months, I had lost 30lbs. It was amazing.'

Some of the participants who took part in the study were not full-time workers, and some had opted to do a lot of their treatment outside of work. This showed that it is possible to access these treatments even if you are on a low income.

Self-Hypnosis Techniques

I will acquaint you with a straightforward, however powerful strategy of self-spellbinding. This procedure is called eye obsession self-entrancing and is one of the most mainstream and successful types of self-spellbinding at any point created. We will begin by utilizing it as a technique to enable you to unwind. After you have rehearsed these various occasions, we will include entrancing recommendations and symbolism. Decrease interruptions by going into a room where you are probably not going to be upset and killing your telephone, TV, PC, and so on. It is your time. You are going to concentrate on your objective of self-entrancing, and that's it.

At that point:

Sit In An Agreeable Seat With Your Legs And Feet Uncrossed

Abstain from eating a huge feast not long previously, so you don't feel enlarged or awkward. Unless you want to fall asleep, please sit in your seat because resting in bed may prompt you to rest. You may likewise want to extricate intimate apparel and remove your shoes. If you wear contact focal points, it is prudent to expel them.

 Keep your legs and feet uncrossed.

Gaze Toward The Roof And Take In A Full Breath
Without applying pressure to the neck or tilting the head back, choose a point on the roof and fix the appearance to that point. When you focus on this point, hold your breath for one second, and then breathe in again. Quietly rehash the recommendation, "my eyes are damage and substantial, and I need to sleep now." rehash this procedure to yourself another couple of times and, if your eyes have not effectively done as such, let them close and

unwind in a typical shut position. It is significant when saying the recommendation that you express it to yourself as though you mean it, for instance, is a delicate, mitigating, however persuasive way.

Allow Your Body To Unwind

Permit your body to turn out to be free and limp in the seat only like a cloth doll. At that point, gradually and with goal tally down quietly from five to zero. Disclose to yourself that with every single check, you're turning out to be increasingly loose. Remain in this relaxed state for various minutes while concentrating on your relaxation. Note the rise and fall of the abdomen and chest. Know how slack your body will become in any situation, try and relax it. In fact, the less you try, the more relaxed you believe.

At The Point When Prepared, Return To The Room By Checking Up From One To Five

Disclose to yourself that you are getting mindful of your environmental factors, and at the tally of five, you will open your eyes. Tally up from one to five out of an exuberant, enthusiastic way. At the enumeration of five, open your eyes and stretch your arms and legs.
Rehash this procedure three or multiple times and notice how each time you arrive at a more profound degree of unwinding. I hope to absorb the information contained in it, so I am determined to practice self-improvement all the time.
Some of the time, individuals will feel somewhat scattered or sluggish after they come out of the charming. It is like arising from an evening snooze, which is innocuous and goes after a couple of seconds. Be that as it may, don't drive or work hardware until you feel entirely wakeful.

Different Levels Of Brain Activity

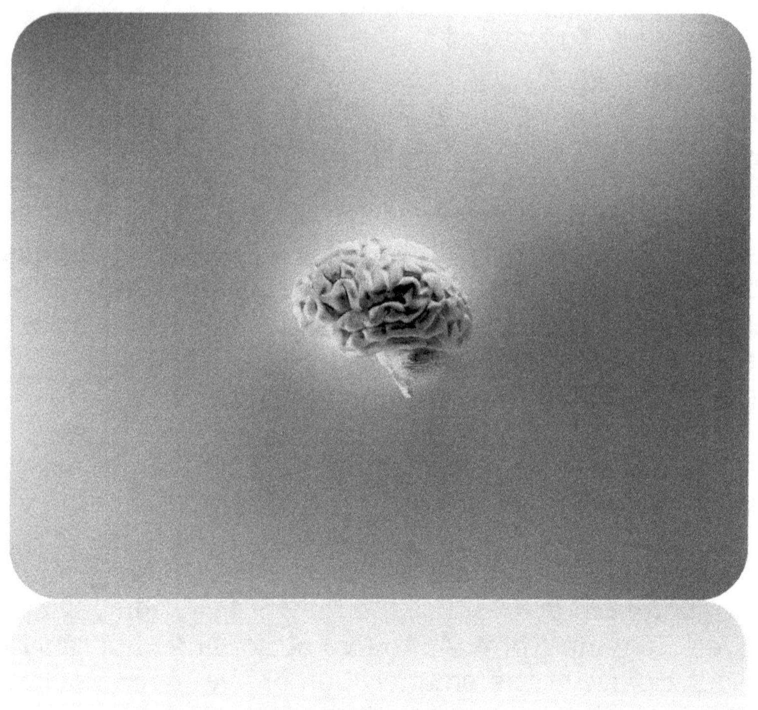

Our brain is an entirely fantastic tool! It is made up of several billion cells that exchange information. These exchanges cause the emission of weak electrical currents - brain waves that can be captured by the electroencephalogram. The rhythm of these waves (measured in cycles per second) varies according to our activity: awakening, learning, rest, relaxation, light sleep, deep sleep.

The Beta Rhythm

It is the cycle of full awakening, the one we work on when we have our eyes open, and we are in action, we reflect, study, learn, etc. Our brain then works in full throttle, and the encephalogram shows us that it shows cycles in the range of 14 to 21 cycles per second. In hyper-activity states, our brains function much closer to 21 cycles/seconds than 14 processes.

The Alpha Rhythm

As soon as we have our eyes closed, we take a comfortable position, lying on a bed; for example, automatically, the encephalogram shows a slowing of brain waves, and our brain then operates at a rate that oscillates between 7 and 14 cycles/seconds.
It is interesting to note that at this rate, the two hemispheres of the brain manage to function together in perfect harmony whereas, during the Beta rhythm, we often operate with a dominant hemisphere (the left in most cases), which privileges analytical work and reflection but which "deprives" us of all the intuitive, creative and global perception of the right hemisphere.
But we'll go back a little further on the benefits of the Alpha rhythm.

The Rhythm Of Theta

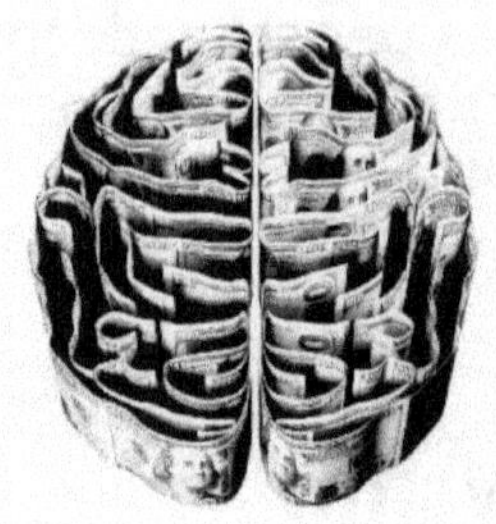

When brain activity slows down further, and we arrive in an area that oscillates between 4 and 7 cycles/seconds, we can say that the brain works at the rate of Theta waves. This rhythm corresponds to the phase of light sleep, and the deeper we sink into this rhythm, the deeper the rest becomes. At the Theta level, we also find the area corresponding to guided hypnosis and the size of pain insensitivity. It is, therefore, this level that we explore during deep hypnosis and regression sessions, and also that which is used in hospitals for anesthesia hypnosis.

The Delta Rhythm

It corresponds to the area of the unconscious, profound sleep, and the more we operate below four cycles/seconds, the more we fall into coma states that approach physical death. In this area, only vital functions are performed by the brain. When the encephalogram shows a flat path, it means brain death no longer had brain activity, and the individual is considered physically dead.

What Is So Special About The Alpha Level?

Let's go back to the alpha wave cycle, which we are particularly interested in since we can reach it alone through meditation, which is more difficult for the theta level, for which we need to be guided so as not to fall into sleep.

Why is this cycle essential to us? When we operate at alpha cerebral rhythm, our mind is calmer, and the two hemispheres of our brain function in perfect harmony (instead of usually having the rational left brain dominating), allowing us to have a more global view of things, which still allows us to:

·   To have a better concentration.
·   To have a better memory.
·   To be able to manage our stress and emotional states better.
·   to be able to take conscious control of the functioning of our bodies, organs, and physiological reactions.
·   to be able to take control of our habits, especially those we want to change.

·   To be able to create new, more positive, and healthy habits for our lives,
·   To find more creative and constructive solutions to conflicts or problems.
At the alpha level, we have a better perception of all our senses, and we are much more attuned to our intuition, which means that we know better what to do when we need to do it. Our mind is then "watchful" it interferes less often, and our choice is then fairer, more intuitive Intuition can be defined as this ability to know information that is outside our usual field of perception. She then communicates her messages to us through images, perceptions, voices.

The Four Alpha Level Sub-Levels

The alpha rhythm also breaks down into four levels:-
Level 4, very close to the state of awakening, activates automatically as soon as one takes a comfortable position, either comfortably installed in an armchair, or lying on a bed, and closes one's eyes. At that point, our brain automatically slows down brain waves. Then, if we persist longer, we feel our whole body relax. It's level 3 of the alpha rhythm.

At Level 3, our mind is still very active; we are still able to think of ten thousand things that concern us, then comes the moment when we feel like we're hovering. To be fair, we would be almost unable at that time to know what we were thinking is Level 2.

Then just after this phase, we sink a little more; we go through level 1, the necessary level of the alpha rhythm. Without even realizing it and because we are not aware of it, we fall even lower asleep. There are brain already works in Theta, and it's a shame because just before that, the opportunity was given to us at level 1, the necessary level of the alpha rhythm, to open the door of our subconscious and give him particular orders so that it serves us instead of helping us, as he often does.

The purpose of exercises and methods of cognitive control at the alpha level, such as the Silva Method or personal active meditation exercises, aims to learn to reach level 1, to master it while regularly maintaining control and without falling further down in sleep. You could almost say that this is a sports exercise, although here the sport is purely cerebral. If I make this comparison with a joke, it is not entirely innocent because, as you know, the athletic performance will be directly proportional to the training you have done. So the more you train to work consciously at the alpha level, the easier it will be and the more valuable benefits you will get in all areas of your life:

·   To improve your health

- To set professional goals and achieve them
- To work on your self-confidence
- To strengthen and develop your intuition
- To quit smoking
- Losing weight, etc.

Challenges Learning Self-Hypnosis

The harder you attempt to recollect the title, the harder it is to review. At that point, when you loosen up, the character returns to you. In some cases, when we make a decent attempt, we square ourselves from accomplishing our objectives. The mentality you take towards self-entrancing will decide how effectively you learn it. Acknowledge the pace at which you accomplish results, anyway little they may form the start appear. Have faith in yourself, and you will proceed to make the progress you want.

Post-Hypnotic Suggestions And Their Rules

As recently referenced, spellbinding is a condition of uplifted suggestibility. Giving yourself proposals when entrancing will empower an activity or other reaction to happen after the mesmerizing experience has happened. These types of recommendations are called post-mesmerizing suggestions and will assist you in achieving your objectives. Throughout the years, subliminal specialists have created rules of request. These are rules that will empower you to make the most significant progress with the proposals you give yourself. What follows is a synopsis of these principles.

Will Gastric Band Hypnotherapy Work For Me?

There are numerous diverse kinds of hypnosis that aid the human body in different ways. Some of these methods include hypnosis for weight loss and healthy living, which are different types of hypnosis for weight loss. Gastric band hypnotherapy is one of them, and popularly known as a type of hypnotic state that is suggested to your subconscious, which involves fitting a gastric band around your stomach. This in return, helps you lose weight, along with general hypnosis for weight loss sessions.

This type of hypnotherapy is often considered the final type of hypnotherapy people try if they would like to reach their goals. The practice involves surgery known as gastric band surgery. During surgery, a gastric band gets fitted around the upper part of your stomach, with the purpose to limit the total amount of food you consume daily. This is a more extreme type of hypnotherapy for weight loss, which has proven to help people lose weight. Since it is surgical, you cannot carry out this method yourself. It also includes potential risks, which is why it must be treated with respect and only carried out by a certified medical practitioner.

You can, however, implement gastric band hypnotherapy yourself. It is a technique most commonly used by hypnotherapists with the purpose to trick the subconscious into believing that a gastric band has been fitted when in reality it hasn't. Since hypnotherapy is focused on putting your conscious mind on silent, and implementing thoughts and beliefs in your subconscious mind, as a type of hypnotherapy, it is quite effective. Given that hypnotherapy offers us many benefits, as well as allows us to imagine and come to terms with what we are capable of doing, it acts as the perfect solution to reaching some of your goals that may seem out of reach.

Gastric band hypnotherapy involves the process of believing that you have experienced the physical surgery itself, ultimately making you believe that the size of your stomach itself has been reduced too.

The gastric band used in gastric band fitting surgery is an adjustable silicone structure, used as a device to lose weight. This gastric band is used during surgery and placed strategically around the top part of your stomach, leaving a small space above the device. The space left open above the gastric band restricts the total amount of food that is stored inside the stomach. This is done to implement proper portion control every day and prevents overeating. The fitted gastric band physically makes it difficult for one to consume large amounts of food, which can set you in the habit of implementing proper portion control daily. This will essentially cause you to feel fuller after eating less, which in return encourages weight loss.

Most people choose to have the surgery after they've tried other methods to lose weight, including yo-yo dieting, diet supplements, or over-the-counter drugs, all with the hope to lose weight. Gastric band surgery acts as a final resort for those who desperately want to lose weight and have been struggling for a long time.

Gastric band hypnotherapy serves as a very useful method as it can allow you to obtain a similar result as the gastric band fitting surgery itself. That's because you are literally visualizing getting the same procedure done and how you benefit from it. During gastric band hypnosis, you are visualizing yourself losing weight subconsciously, which translates into your conscious reality.

Hypnotherapists that specialize in gastric band hypnotherapy focus on finding the root of what prevents their clients from losing weight. Most of the time, they discover that emotional eating is one of the leading causes that contribute to people holding on to their weight. They also make a point of addressing experiences that remains in your subconscious mind but is yet to be addressed.

These experiences often cause people to turn toward unmindful and emotional eating, which then develops into a pattern that feels impossible to kick.

Since stress is added to our lives every day, and people don't stop and take the time to process feelings or perhaps not even give them a thought, most turn to food for comfort. This also plays into emotional eating, which has extremely negative effects on the body long-term as it also contributes as one of the leading causes of obesity.

Given that obesity is an incredibly bad illness, and more people get diagnosed with the condition every day, it is something that needs to be addressed. If gastric band hypnotherapy can prevent it or restructure our thinking patterns to not act on our emotions, but rather invite and process it, then it is a solution that everyone who needs to lose weight should try.

Once a hypnotherapist learns about why you're struggling to implement proper portion control, they will address it with the virtual gastric band treatment at a subconscious level. During this visualization session, you will have imagined that you have undergone the operation and had the gastric band placed around your upper stomach. This will lead you to think that you feel fuller quicker, serving as a safer option as opposed to the surgery.

How Gastric Band Hypnotherapy Works

Hypnotherapy for weight loss, particularly for portion control, is great because it allows you to focus on creating a healthier version of yourself safely.

When gastric band-fitted surgery gets recommended to people, usually because diets, weight loss supplements, and workout routines don't seem to work for them, they may become skeptical about getting the surgery done. Nobody wants to undergo unnecessary surgery, and you shouldn't have to either. Just because you struggle to stick to a diet, workout routine or lack motivation does not mean that an extreme procedure like surgery is the only option. In fact, thinking that it is the only option you have left, is crazy.

Some hypnotherapists suggest that diets don't work at all. Well, if you're motivated and find it easy to stick to a diet plan and workout routine, then you should be fine. However, if you're suffering from obesity or overweight and don't have the necessary drive and motivation needed, then you're likely to fail. When people find the courage and determination to recognize that they need to lose weight or actually push themselves to do it but continuously fail, that's when they tend to give up.

Gastric band hypnotherapy uses relaxation techniques, which are designed to alter your way of thinking about the weight you need to lose, provides you a foundation to stand on and reach your goals, and also constantly reminds you of why you're indeed doing what you're doing. It is necessary to develop your way of thinking past where you're at in this current moment and evolve far beyond your expectations.

Diets are also more focused on temporary lifestyle changes rather than permanent and sustainable ones, which is why it isn't considered realistic at all. Unless you change your mind, you will always remain in a rut that involves first losing, and then possibly gaining weight back repeatedly. Some may even throw in the towel completely.

Since your mind is incredibly powerful, it will allow you to accept any ideas or suggestions made during your hypnosis gastric band hypnosis session. This can result in changing your behavior permanently as the ideas practiced during the session will translate into the reality of your conscious mind. By educating yourself on healthy habits, proper nutrition, and exercise, you also stand a better chance of reaching your weight loss goals sustainably.

The gastric band fitting procedure will require a consultation with your hypnotherapist where you will discuss what it is you would like to gain from hypnotherapy. After establishing your current health status, positive and negative habits, lifestyle, daily struggles, and goals, they will recommend the duration of hypnotherapy you will require to see results. During this time, you need to inform your hypnotherapist of your diet and physical activity history. They are likely to ask you questions about your current lifestyle and whether you changed it over the years. If you've lived a healthy lifestyle before, then they will try to find and address the reasons why you let go of yourself and your health. If you have always lived your current unhealthy and unbalanced lifestyle, they will trace it back through the years with the hope to discover the reasons behind it. During your initial session, your weight loss attempts, eating habits, and any health issues you may experience will be addressed. Your attitude toward food will also be acknowledged, as well as your relationship with it, with people, and your surroundings.

Now your therapist will have a better idea of the type of treatment you need. The procedure is designed to have you experience the gastric band surgery subconsciously, as though it has really taken place. You will be talked to in a deep, relaxed state, exactly the same as standard hypnosis. During this session, you will be aware of everything happening around you. Suggestions to help boost your self-esteem and confidence are often also incorporated into the session, which can also assist you in what you would like to achieve consciously.

You will be taken through the procedure step-by-step. Your hypnotherapist may also make theater noises to convince your subconscious even more. After your session, your hypnotherapist may give you self-hypnosis guides and techniques to help you practice a similar session for the results to become more effective. Sometimes, gastric band hypnotherapy only requires a few sessions, depending on what your needs are.

Gastric band hypnosis doesn't only involve having to go to physical hypnotherapy sessions, but it also requires you to implement some type of weight management program that specifically addresses your nutrition, addiction, and exercise habits. It addresses habits between your body and mind and helps you implement new constructive ones.

After gastric band hypnosis, you can expect to feel as though you have a much healthier relationship with food, as well as a more mindful approach in everything you do. During the visualization process of gastric band fitting surgery, you will come to believe that your stomach has shrunk, which will trick your brain into thinking that you need less food. This will also make you think that you don't need a lot of food, which will make you more acquainted with consuming healthier portion sizes.

Gastric band hypnotherapy is successful as it makes you think that you are full after eating the daily recommended amount of food for your body. It is also considered much healthier than overeating or binge eating. You will learn to recognize the sensation of hunger versus being full, which will help you articulate between the two and cultivate healthier eating habits.

Self-Hypnosis For The Sense Of Safety

(put music with binaural sounds)

Choose a quiet, noise-free environment.

Sit or lie down comfortably.

Close your eyes.

(pause 3 seconds)

Make contact with the breath.

Allow my voice to guide you through this process.

(pause 5 seconds)

Inhale through your nostrils, mentally counting to three.

One.

Two.

Three.

Hold your breath.

Exhale from the nostrils, mentally counting to four.

One.

Two.

Three.

Four.

(pause 5 seconds)

Inhale and mentally repeat: "While inhaling, I relax" and
meanwhile observe the flow of breath.
(pause 5 seconds)

Exhale and mentally repeat: "While I exhale, I relax" and
meanwhile observe the flow of breath.

(pause 5 seconds)

Inhale and mentally repeat: "As I inhale, I relax more and
more" and in the meantime listen to the sound of
breathing.

(pause 5 seconds)

Exhale and mentally repeat: "As I exhale, I relax more and
more" and meanwhile listen to the sound of breathing.

(pause 5 seconds)

As you inhale, repeat mentally: "As I breathe in, I relax
even more" and meanwhile I contract the muscles of my
arms and legs.

(pause 5 seconds)

As you exhale, mentally repeat: "While I exhale, I relax
even more" and meanwhile relax the muscles of the arms
and legs.

(pause 5 seconds)

There is a door in front of you.

You open it.

Exit the door and you're on a beach.

(pause 10 seconds)

The sky is blue, cloudless. Feel the sound of the light wind.
See the seagulls sliding in the air.

(pause 5 seconds)

The sand is white, warm underfoot.

(pause 5 seconds)

Look at the sea. It is calm, serene, peaceful.

(pause 5 seconds)

As you watch it, you also feel calm, peaceful, calm.

(pause 5 seconds)

You start walking on the beach, towards the water. You feel the warm sand under your toes and you feel satisfied, you feel satisfied.

(pause 5 seconds)

Inhale deeply through your nose. Feel the scent of salt and sea. It fills you with freshness.

(pause 5 seconds)

It satisfies your body, mind, and soul.

(pause 5 seconds)

You came to the water. Feel the wet sand and then the water that caresses your feet and ankles. It is warm and soft like sand.

(pause 5 seconds)

Even the waves have a soft, sweet, satisfying sound.

(pause 5 seconds)

Each wave that melts on the sand satisfies you even more. It satisfies you even more.

(pause 5 seconds)

When the wave withdraws, your dissatisfaction withdraws.

(pause 5 seconds)

You start taking a walk along the beach and enjoy every step you take.

(pause 5 seconds)

You keep walking and you enjoy every sensation.

(pause 5 seconds)

There is nobody on the beach except you and you feel perfectly at ease.

(pause 5 seconds)

In front of you see a large, comfortable mattress.

(pause 3 seconds)

You can't wait to lie down.

(pause 2 seconds)

You can't wait to savor the pleasure of total fulfillment.

(pause 3 seconds)

You lie down on the large and comfortable mattress and immediately savor the feelings of joy and well-being.

(pause 5 seconds)

You continue to enjoy the sound of the wind and waves.

Continue to enjoy the softness of the mattress.

Continue to enjoy the delight of this moment.

(pause 5 seconds)

You always feel happier.

More and more satisfied.

More and more satisfied.

(pause 5 seconds)

You hear the sound of the waves, and every wave that arrives on the beach satisfies you more and more. It satisfies your body.

It satisfies your mind.

You are satisfied with the spirit.

(pause 10 seconds)

Bring attention to the head.

(pause 5 seconds)

Feel how the whole head is completely satisfied.

Sated.

Satisfied.

Of this being here and now.

You don't need anything.

(pause 5 seconds)

Open your mouth slightly and let the jaw relax.
Your mouth is full.

Your language is full.

Your throat is full.

You don't need anything.

(pause 5 seconds)

Bring attention to your arms.

Feel how they are loose, stretched, from shoulders to fingers.

Do you feel OK?

You do not need anything.

(pause 5 seconds)

Bring attention to your legs.

Relax them even more.

(pause 5 seconds)

Bring attention to your back.

Feel how loose, relaxed, from the neck to the buttocks.

You always feel better.

You realize that you need nothing more than this well-being.

(pause 5 seconds)

Bring attention to your chest.

Let her relax even more.

(pause 5 seconds)

Bring attention to the stomach.

It is sated. Joyful. Happy.

(pause 5 seconds)

Bring attention to the abdomen.

It feeds on this feeling.

Of this well-being.

Of this pleasure.

(pause 10 seconds)

Enjoy the well-being of being free from every need.

(pause 5 seconds)

Enjoy the pleasure of being satisfied.

In the body.

In the mind.

In the soul.

(pause 5 seconds)

Your every cell feeds on well-being.

Your every cell is satisfied.

Satisfied.

Satisfied.

(pause 5 seconds)

You are satisfied.

Satisfied.

Satisfied.

(pause 5 seconds)

Understand now your wonderful well-being.

(pause 5 seconds)

You are like this beach, these waves, this mattress.

(pause 5 seconds)

You are a satisfied and satisfied person in any situation.

(pause 5 seconds)

Feel how easy it is to let go of all your worries and needs.
(pause 5 seconds)

Feel how easy it is to be satiated and satisfied.

(pause 5 seconds)

Continue to feel the sense of satiety.

(pause 5 seconds)

The sense of satiety expands in your body, in your mind, in your soul.

(pause 5 seconds)

The sense of satiety pervades every hour.

Every minute.

Every second of your day.

(pause 5 seconds)

Prepare now to enter an even deeper fulfillment state.

Get ready to make this feeling of perfect satiety your main feeling.

(pause 5 seconds)

Continue to lie on the soft mattress of this sweet beach.

(pause 5 seconds)

Now the sun is about to set on the horizon.

(pause 5 seconds)

Observe the line of the sea that meets the sun in the distance: as the sun sets, I will count from ten to one. When I get to one, the sun will be completely set and you will be completely and perfectly satisfied.
Completely and perfectly satisfied.

Ten

The sun begins to set on the horizon. Note how the colors change, while the sun begins to drop: note the orange of the sky, the blue and green of the water, how they mix together. Your feeling of well-being mixes with these colors.

Nine

The sun goes down on the horizon and you feel full of well-being.

You feel yourself floating in this well-being.

Eight

The sunsets behind the horizon and you feel the sense of satiety descending in the mouth, in the tongue, in the throat.

Seven

The sense of satiety descends into the chest, stomach, abdomen.

Six

The colors still change. The water is now a calm golden mirror and you feel this way too.

Calm and bright. You are confidently abandoning yourself to the current.

Five

The sense of satiety descends into the pelvis, genitals, legs.

Every part of your body lets itself go more and more to this sense of satiety.

Four

As the sun goes down more and more, you feel this perfect sense of satiety throughout your body from the tip of your head to the tip of your feet.

Three

You are completely at peace.

Two

Float in this sense of satiety.

One

You keep floating in this sense of satiety.

(pause 5 seconds)

With this satiety, it is easy for you to lose excess weight. Because now you know you don't need to eat more.

(pause 5 seconds)

Now you know it's not the food that satisfies you.

Now you know that what satisfies you is this well-being.

(pause 5 seconds)

Now you know it's not the food that relaxes you.

What relaxes you is this well-being.

(pause 5 seconds)

Now you know it's not the food that gives you security.

What gives you security is this well-being.

(pause 5 seconds)

Now you know that it is not the food that satisfies your needs.

What satisfies your needs is this well-being.

(pause 5 seconds)

Now you know it because you know it.

You know why you feel it.

Why do you live it?

(pause 5 seconds)

You will bring this satiety and this sense of well-being into your life and with this satiety, from now on, it will be easy for you to maintain the right weight.

(pause 5 seconds)

Continue to float in this sense of well-being and satiety.

Feel how this sense of well-being and satiety is part of you.

Feel how this sense of well-being and satiety is you.

(pause 5 seconds)

Now bring this feeling of perfect satiety into your everyday life.

Join the index and thumb of the right hand and the left hand.

Anchor the feeling of perfect satiety to this finger gesture and bring it into your life.

(pause 10 seconds)

Keep holding your index fingers and thumbs together and allow this feeling of perfect satiety to flow through you.
(pause 10 seconds)

Whenever you join your index fingers and thumbs together in your waking state, you will instantly reactivate this feeling of perfect satiety and you will feel it flowing in you instantly.

(pause 5 seconds)

Whenever you feel the feeling of hunger outside ordinary meals, you will join your index fingers and thumbs and instantly reactivate this feeling of perfect satiety.

So you will feel perfectly satisfied, instantly.

(pause 10 seconds)

From now on, in the waking state, you will spontaneously associate the sense of hunger with this gesture, which will instantly satisfy you.

Separate your index fingers and thumbs.

(pause 5 seconds)

You are about to return to the waking state.

Prepare to bring every word you have heard and every feeling you have to wakefulness.

(pause 5 seconds)

Your subconscious mind will process every word you have heard and bring it into your everyday life.

(pause 5 seconds)

You will want to listen to this audio and every time you hear these words, the suggestion will become more and more powerful for you.

(pause 5 seconds)

Whenever you hear these words again, the suggestion will become an increasingly important part of you.

(pause 5 seconds)

Every time you hear these words again, you will become more and more the person you have chosen to be.

(pause 5 seconds)

Mentally repeat:

 "I will count from one to five and at the end of the count I will feel completely awake and better than before."

(pause 5 seconds)

One.

(pause 3 seconds)

Two.

Mentally repeat:

"I am about to return to the waking state, which means that even in the waking state my subconscious will continue to carry out the instructions I have given it."

(pause 5 seconds)

Three.

Repeat mentally: "Soon I will open my eyes."

(pause 3 seconds)

Four.

Repeat mentally: "Every day I will feel more satisfied and satisfied".

(pause 5 seconds)

Five.

Open your eyes.
You are now fully awake, feeling good, feeling better than before.

(Turn off the music with binaural sounds)

Final tips

Remember to repeat this self-hypnosis constantly following
the program. The subconscious works out of habit and
habit are formed with repetition. Repetition is therefore
essential for the program to work in the best way.

I also suggest that you immediately test the functioning of
the anchor. Put your index fingers and thumbs together
and feel the sensation of satiety flowing inside you.
It must be activated clearly, you must have full sensation.

Hypnotherapy and Insomnia/Sleep Problems

In minimizing or treating insomnia, hypnotherapy may be very effective, although not all forms of insomnia are vulnerable to hypnotic care. Hypnotherapy may not respond well to insomnia induced by biological disorder, sickness, or medication effects. However, if the key causes of your insomnia are stress and anxiety, then hypnosis, together with proper sleep hygiene, can well provide an efficient cure.

Sleep Hypnosis

What is Insomnia?

Sleep is something that everybody needs. In both our physical and mental wellbeing, it plays a crucial part. But sleeping disorders, such as insomnia, can make having enough sleep difficult for certain people. Lack of sleep, as well as making you feel exhausted, will lead to physical illness, and increase the risk of heart disease. Mentally, not having enough sleep will lead to anxiety and make focus difficult for you.

Insomnia is described as trouble trying to sleep or remaining asleep long enough for the next morning to feel refreshed.

When you can't manage to fall asleep, most of us will have experienced a night of disturbed sleep and will know how it feels. You may be worried for the next day or you may have had a cup too close to bedtime. You might find it easy to fall asleep, but you keep waking up at night. A tough sleep will leave you feeling exhausted and irritable the next day, either way. Many who suffer from insomnia will frequently feel these emotions. A third of individuals in the UK are reported to have bouts of insomnia throughout their lives. While it can influence anyone at any age, it seems that individuals over the age of 60 and women are more vulnerable.

Different Types of Insomnia

There are several distinct forms of insomnia, but they are commonly grouped into two categories:

1.   **Temporary Insomnia**
When it lasts between one night and three to four weeks, insomnia is known as transient or acute.
Jet lag, a shift of schedule or working environments, stress, caffeine, and alcohol are typical causes of transient insomnia.
Transient or sporadic insomnia is the name of certain examples of temporary insomnia. This is where the person occasionally develops sleeping difficulties over months or years.

2.   **Persistent Insomnia**
This is considered chronic insomnia as well. The problem would usually continue almost nightly, for a period of four weeks. This may also occur as sleep is disturbed by pain or treatment from medical conditions. This may include arthritis, Parkinson's disease, asthma, allergies, chemicals that change, or concerns with mental health.

Symptoms Of Insomnia

Based on specific conditions, signs vary. There are common symptoms, however, including:

- keeping up at night for long hours.

- Not being conscious of falling asleep.

- Waking up during the night several times.

- Waking up very early and being unable to sleep again.

- Feeling exhausted the next morning and groggy.

- Finding it impossible to focus or work correctly.

- The sense of irritability.

Causes of Insomnia

The problem has multiple possible sources. In certain cases, sleeplessness may be caused by only one cause, while others may undergo a mixture of variables.
Any of insomnia's possible causes include:

Conditions in Physical Fitness

If you suffer from a health issue that causes you discomfort, you can find falling asleep difficult.
Likewise, if you have a disease, like asthma, that affects your breathing. It is assumed that sleep cycles can also be caused by hormone disorders and urinary conditions.
There is a risk your sleep will be disturbed by the medicine you are taking. Talk to the doctor if you suspect a health condition or think that your medicine can trigger a problem with your sleep.

Mental Health Conditions

Sleeping issues may be created by such mental health conditions. An individual with extreme depression, for instance, is more likely to suffer from insomnia. When a person loses sleep, the depressed moods that come with depression may also be exacerbated.
Another disorder that is often associated with insomnia is anxiety. Anxiety may cause an entity to feel tense, worried, and exhausted. These emotions can find it difficult to fall asleep. When trying to sleep, the mind of the person will always run, feeling as though they cannot "switch off."
Sleep can also be disrupted by the concern and the person

may wake up in the night. The anxiety about not having enough sleep will turn into a vicious circle if this trend continues.

Lifestyle

Sleeping behaviors may be affected by everyday activities and lifestyles. For starters, if you drink alcohol daily, you can find that during the night you wake up. Alcohol is a stimulant and even after taking a few drinks it can appear easy to fall asleep, it typically contributes to bad sleep overall.

Drugs and caffeine can similarly lead to issues with sleep. Any addiction to drugs is going to affect how you sleep, so it is important to seek help. It is advised that you minimize the consumption of caffeine if you suffer from insomnia. Worked late into the night will find it impossible to turn off the brain. For your internal clock, shift work will create chaos and make sleeping tricky. It could be worth reassessing your hours if your job (or work-related stress) is affecting your insomnia.

The Way Insomnia Works

People with insomnia also say they are "insomniacs"; that is, genetically predisposed to insomnia.
There should be nothing farther from the facts. There is a dormant time in any living organism, so sleep is normal, so insomnia is unnatural.
Insomnia in general is caused by an intrinsic fear that may be about families, economic problems, questions of self-esteem, and numerous other anxieties. Every single client is different. However, we can figure out what is happening and fix the symptoms at a subconscious level by using hypnotherapy for Insomnia, bringing you back to a normal sleep cycle.
"Almost 30 percent of the population has a sort of sleeplessness. Anxiety almost always underpins insomnia, and this anxiety interrupts the normal rhythm of sleep. This fear is something persons with insomnia appear to ruminate on when going to sleep, which is what hypnotherapy targets with insomnia. This rumination produces elevated levels of anxiety and hence, within the insomniac, an elevated degree of alertness and therefore sleep eludes them. This anxiety is often so poor that the client might not be really conscious of it and thus assumes that there is little cause for the loss of sleep. Paul White, the insomnia specialist at the Surrey Institute of Clinical Hypnotherapy.

Treatment For Insomnia

There are different methods you might take when treating sleeping issues. In order to remove all physical triggers, it is necessary to first talk to the doctor. To help you sleep, your doctor can prescribe that you take medication. This may be an efficient therapy for certain persons, but it is necessary to try to figure out the root cause of the problem. Behavioral therapies and voice therapies are also suggested.

Another treatment choice which many people find successful is hypnotherapy. Insomnia hypnotherapy can resolve the possible triggers while helping you relax and go to sleep. For example, if the cause of your insomnia is anxiety or depression, sleep hypnosis can supplement your established therapy. It can then help to change the sleeping routine by solving these problems.

Alternatively, hypnotherapy for insomnia will work to break this habit if a habit causes your insomnia (such as alcohol).

As the suggestions made by hypnosis therapy allow your mind and body to relax and get the sleep you need the worry, discomfort, and fear that can prevent you from falling asleep fade away.

Ogunyemi Biodun

Hypnotherapy For Sleep

Although there may be an apparent reason for some sleeping issues, others will not. If you are unclear whether you are having trouble sleeping, hypnotherapy for insomnia may be beneficial. A hypnotherapist can reach into the subconscious using multiple methods to discover what could have caused the issue. A personalized therapy developed by the hypnotherapist will begin after the cause is identified.

The habits of sleep disturbances will become ingrained in the subconscious when suffering from insomnia for a long period of time. The aim of hypnosis for insomnia is to engage with it and propose constructive changes. These suggestions will aim to break the habits of negative thinking that trigger the problem.

Teaching you how to relax is an essential aspect of hypnotherapy for insomnia. Physical or emotional stress can make sleeping uncomfortable for certain individuals. To help relieve anxiety, a hypnotherapist can use relaxing methods, such as gradual muscle relaxation.

A hypnotherapist will also teach you self-hypnosis. It will help you create a schedule, as well as learn how to deal with the problem triggering the causes. Using hypnosis at home for insomnia will help you put into your daily life the techniques you have gained in the session room.

What Exactly Is Sleep Hypnosis?

If there was an easy and risk-free sleep aid that you might use daily, wouldn't it be a dream? Well, there is one, and it's called hypnosis of sleep! Hypnosis has been a well-known calming and implicit suggestion method for well over a century. The increasing use of this mystical self-improvement approach has been ignited by the use of sleep hypnosis for stopping cigarettes, treating chronic pain, curing insomnia, and more.

Sleep hypnosis is used by certain individuals as a technique to make them fall asleep. Sleep hypnosis, in a nutshell, is a procedure that requires directed thought to lead a person into a state of relaxation.

This comfortable state could, in fact, make it easier to fall asleep. Several types of sleep hypnosis available can be downloaded to your phone or device, although it is not certain whether they are accurate or not. Read on for information about what it is, whether you are trying sleep hypnosis, and find other techniques that may be more effective when you want to get a decent night's sleep.

Sleep hypnosis is a session through which a hypnotherapist directs a participant by verbal gestures to cause calm and a trance that may be used to help you drift to sleep, either in person or by a video.

Hypnosis helps the recipient to actively "sleep" while still subconsciously aware. The ensuing trancelike state happens with the delta, theta, alpha states of lower-level brainwave activation where conscious activity subsides, and subconscious activity rises. It is also possible to use sleep hypnosis to bring the listener into deep and restorative sleep.

Sleep hypnosis requires listening to a hypnotherapist's auditory signals that are meant to draw you by the force of persuasion into a trance-like condition. Hypnotherapists use multiple techniques, such as concentrated concentration, control of symptoms, and directed visualization, to promote relief.

A person who is hypnotized can hear phrases like "relax," "deep," "easy," and let go." These words are supposed to encourage someone to drift off to sleep.

A hypnosis session for sleep includes:

Settling down: The receiver lies down and gets settled.

Letting go The listener is directed to place aside any doubts or concerns.

Induction: By relaxing the conscious mind and opening up the subconscious, it prepares the listener to go further into relaxation.

Breathing: This segment requires deliberate breathing that takes the recipient into equilibrium even more intensely.

The suggestion: This entails directed visualization that plants the intended outcome into the subconscious mind of the listener, the longest and final part of the hypnosis.

You may be curious whether wishful thinking is hypnosis or if it works. Fortunately, there is considerable research on the subject of sleep hypnosis.

Conclusion

What specifically makes it so difficult for a woman to lose weight. To start off with, it is not uncommon for women to be carrying more fat than men are, which could be as much as twelve kilograms (26lbs). This weighs down on her system and is causing the body to hold on tightly to fat stores and calories. In this case, the more weight you have to lose, the harder it may be to lose.

Another fact that adds to the difficulty of women losing weight is that they're simply not as active as men are. It is unreasonable for a woman to expect herself to burn off fat by exercising too much. Yes, she needs to exercise every day, but she should make sure she doesn't overdo it.

It could be beneficial if your wife or girlfriend took up a plan such as gastric band hypnosis rapid weight loss. This will allow her diet plan and exercise program to be holistic in the sense that it deals with not only what she eats but also how much and how often she exercises. This will put the best possible weight loss plan into play and will make it easier for her to drop pounds.

As with all diet programs, there are certain restrictions that need to be adhered to in order for them to be effective. For instance, a woman needs to have a low-calorie diet that ensures she is consuming about 700 calories daily (or about 1,800 calories per day). It is also wise for her to exercise regularly but not excessively; she should aim for no more than two hours of exercise on any given day.

Waiting too long on the diet side of things will only result in a short-term weight loss plan and may even cause some adverse health effects. These range from feeling weak to low energy levels to even depression. It is crucial for a woman not to overdo the exercise side of things as well, especially if it means she's exercising while hungry.

The benefits of gastric band hypnosis rapid weight loss are numerous. There's the obvious fact that this will allow your wife or girlfriend to drop weight without much trouble, but there are other benefits as well, such as the fact that this program is holistic in nature and can help her with diet and exercise.

In addition, there are also health benefits that come along with this plan. Unlike certain other diet programs, gastric band hypnosis rapid weight loss does not have any adverse health effects. Although some side effects should be reported, such as dry mouth, they're not as dangerous as other health problems that may result from using other programs.

Finally, the cost-benefit of it, is also significant. It is very affordable, and the overall costs will go down if your wife or girlfriend decides to use it in combination with a gym membership. All in all, gastric band hypnosis rapid weight loss is a great option to help your wife or girlfriend lose weight and keep it off.